Your best kept secret...

secret...

#thetaylormadeway

By Helen Taylor

To Jan
Thank you for your
support
Helen
xx

This book is also dedicated to My Dad.
I love you.

Foreword

When Helen asked me to write this, I was initially incredibly proud and honoured, and then confused and frankly slightly worried!

What do I write?

I have worked with and mentored Helen for some time now, and I can tell you that people like her, don't come around that often.

She has had an BIG impact on my life, as I have on hers, and Helen is the living proof that focus, determination, consistency and the judicious use of the word 'f**k' will get you your dreams.

The journey of writing a book is a hugely personal and emotional one and the fact that she has decided to share her story with you is truly wonderful. If you are reading this looking for inspiration, insight, and humour, then that is what you will find.

Helen is an amazing individual, funny, warm hearted, caring – she has such a drive to succeed that you can't help but be swept along with her.

So – sit back, relax and enjoy her story, She really is one of a kind...

She is your best kept secret...

Richard Crawford Small

Welcome to the little book that will hopefully create some **BIG changes** to the way that you think about beauty, yourself, and life... **Forever.**

This book is dedicated to **YOU** and the you who exists *inside of you*. Because *that's* where you'll find **true beauty.**

In the you, who has **ALWAYS** been there, she just got lost amongst the rubble.

The rubble of failed relationships, the rubble of broken dreams, and the rubble of false promises.

The YOU who knows, that no matter WHAT life has to throw at her, she will always come back stronger.

You know the you who I am talking about so dig deep and find her, it's time to dust her off again!

Please, pull up a chair, and let's get comfortable – It's time for you to meet me – Helen Taylor, ***your best kept secret.***

hello beautiful

Hello. My name is **Helen Taylor** and for the past 30 years or so I have been working within the beauty and aesthetics industry.

I say that with a little smile on my face, because it's always been so much more than that...

If the walls could talk in my clinic, there's certainly a LOT that they'd share with you. From life changing moments through treatments, to the honest advice I have given you.

The first thing that I want to tell you is that I am NOT just another beauty and aesthetics therapist.

I am a businesswoman ...

I am an industry leader...

But I am also SO much more than that...

I am my clients best kept secret.

And my *hope, in writing this book, is that even if you have never met me, I will become* **your** *best kept secret.*

So, exactly who IS Helen Taylor?

**I am the woman who walked out
of an unhappy marriage.**

**I am the woman, who whilst in her twenties
went to get her nails done and experienced a
life changing moment.**

**I am the woman who looked down at her nails and
knew, 'that I can do what she's doing' ...**

I am the woman who, with every fibre of her being knew she needed to change her direction in life and revisited her childhood ambition...

I am the woman who didn't look back.

To some extent those facts, are now just a part of my history.

But entwined in those memories, are some of *my* best kept secrets. And as we work our way through this book, I hope to share those secrets with you, as you dig deep to reveal **your** best secrets.

My tools for a taylormade life...

1. Respect yourself

2. ALWAYS listen to your intuition

3. Make friends with ageing

4. Never let anyone else define you

5. Never be afraid to walk away from anything (or anyone) that doesn't suit you.

Those are my tools for a taylormade life.
What would YOURS be?

Have you ever really thought about that?

I want you to grab a pen, or a pencil and have a go at writing YOUR tools for a taylormade life.

Please don't overthink this (and talk yourself out of it.) Just do it. And then photocopy this page and plaster your tools everywhere.

My tools for a taylormade life are...

1.

2.

3.

4.

5.

CHAPTER ONE

The voice within

The first time I did a 'Hollywood'...
(of the wax variety that is...)

Oh blimey...

I will never (ever) forget that!

I'd say that this is one of my funniest memories in all
of the years that I've run my own business. The
client in question came to see me after having being
given a few instructions over the telephone...

Instructions Helen? Instructions?
What on earth are you on about?

Instructions! You know... about
how to *prepare* for her Hollywood.

Anyway in she walked and...

She had the brightest purple hair that I had *ever* seen...

There, literally right in front of me, was something that can only be described as bright red and wiry... To make matters worse, she had not even attempted to 'trim' that certain area..., so what should have been a relatively straightforward Hollywood, soon became something internally nerve wracking!

As I worked my way through her foliage, I found myself starting to wonder... Was this REALLY the right direction for my business, was this really 'Helen Taylor'?

Your best kept secret #1

If you get that inner feeling that something isn't right for you, chances are that it really ISN'T. Always, always, always LISTEN to your intuition. It will never fail to guide you.

That's exactly what I did by the way –
I listened to MY intuition...

Shortly after this incident, I simply stopped doing
them... Hollywood waxes... (not red wiry clients that is.)

I simply... stopped... doing them.

And life really can be THAT simple. If something doesn't
sit right with you, simply stop doing it.

I applied that same advice to my marriages, and to
anything else that didn't suit me. And it wasn't always
the easy option. Actually – quite the opposite.

There have been times along this journey that I have
sat back and questioned my choices.

Don't be fooled by my gung ho exterior and
mistake that for meaning that I'm... dare I say it...
heartless. Quite the opposite actually. Between
you and I (I can't believe I'm about to share this...)
I am actually quite the 'sensitive'.

Nothing in life has been easy. I've worked my way out of some real hardships. But that is MY *best kept secret... My ability to rise from the ashes.* I wish there was a magic formula and that I could somehow write it down for you.

Truth is, getting on in life isn't easy, and it takes a LOT (and I mean a LOT) of willpower. But if you can somehow, dig deep, and dust off the nonsense, you'll find the YOU who can totally DO this.

Do what, I hear you ask me? Oh you know... Life, love, and... *Everything.*

Self reflection: What (or who) do YOU need to get rid of?

What or who, do you need to get rid of, in order to make your life happier?

From energy vampires to clutter and rubbish. Get rid of anything (or anyone) that no longer serves you. Use the section below to make notes, and then put this book down and go and DO it.

When you clear space in your house, car, office, workspace, friends list and life in general, you find that you are able to think with more clarity and this is incredibly powerful.

Greater clarity leads to better productivity, increased energy levels and can lower stress and anxiety.

We only get a limited time on this earth, and time isn't slowing down for anyone.

Use your space, energy and time wisely.

#justforme...

Make notes **#justforyou** so that you can remember any moments of inspiration, a-ha's and breakthroughs that this chapter gave to you:

_____

_____

_____

_____

_____

_____

_____

_____

_____

_____

Now, be kind to yourself and stand tall – you've got this!

A dash of Taylormade Therapy

Step into the shower and take a great big splodge of shower gel.

Something refreshing, cleansing, perhaps minty?

Then, as you begin to scrub your body, imagine that you are washing away your troubles.

All of the things and the people that you have made a conscious choice you are going to get rid of... scrub them away, and watch them vanish down the plug hole! Poof! Feels GOOD doesn't it?

CHAPTER TWO

When you're feeling rubbish...

I once ran an ad on a dustcart that used to drive around Rugby. It simply said: 'Feeling rubbish?

The ad did brilliantly, and was a real boost to my business. I can remember it making an appearance when I collected my first award at a regional business awards ceremony.

Winning awards is brilliant by the way... I really can't describe how it feels.

I guess I'd describe it as *amazing*... to be presented with some recognition for the blood sweat and tears that has gone into creating things.

But winning awards isn't *everything*.

After getting that first one, I realised that it's the results I get with my clients, that really matters most to me.

One thing that I used to love about going to award ceremonies, was having my late Father there with me, *being proud of me*... His little girl...

My Dad was ...

God, this is difficult.

He was the man that I loved most deeply.

I suppose you could say that I was closer to my Dad than my Mother, and it was him who I wanted to praise me. When he passed he left a void that's indescribable, and in many ways, as much as I want to talk about him and share him with you here, I still find it incredibly hard to deal with.

He died in 2012, so in many ways it's not all *that* long ago. But to me it still feels like yesterday.

Grief, loss, love, the things that affect I suppose, all of us. And no matter how positive you would like to be throughout life, there are just some things that get the better of you.

Your best kept secret #2:

You can't always bounce straight back from things but you can learn to fall in style.

In other words, sometimes in life, we go through something that is just BIGGER than anything we could imagine, and when those times get the best of us, we have to *learn to fall in style.*

When it comes to losing a parent, there's no simple way to 'get over it' – you've just got to *learn to live with it,*

Another lesson that I learned from losing my Father, was that it's okay to sometimes feel RUBBISH.

You don't have to just paint a smile on it, though a dash of red lipstick never hurt anybody... You are ENTITLED to feel like rubbish. you are allowed to have that mood swing.

It's knowing when to climb out of the rubbish that *defines you*.

P.S: can I get a little personal here for a moment? I would just like to say, that I am truly, truly honoured that so many women share their intimate secrets with me. Seriously, when I first set up my therapy couch, I had no idea of the route that it would take me. You've shared, we've talked, and we've laughed and we've cried. I really am so honoured to have met you... and if you're meeting me for the first time here, it's so far been a pleasure.

Self reflection: How do you dispose of YOUR rubbish?

I want you to think back to the last BIG thing that you had to emotionally handle in life. It could have been a breakup, the loss of a loved one, being diagnosed with an illness. How did you handle it?

Maybe you are going through something in this moment.

Are you great at trying to brush things under the carpet? Do you pretend that you're doing okay with things, when really, you feel like SCREAMING?

Then SCREAM and let it out!!

#justforme…

Make notes **#justforyou** so that you can remember any moments of inspiration, a-ha's and breakthroughs that this chapter gave to you:

_____

_____

_____

_____

_____

_____

_____

_____

_____

_____

_____

_____

A blast of taylormade therapy

Run yourself a nice hot bath. Maybe add some lavender or rose to it. Step in, take a deep breath and *relax for a minute.*

Feels amazing doesn't it?

Try to think of... nothing... and just lie there...

Learn to allow your mind to wander. All of those thoughts... And all of those worries... Simply acknowledge them and then let be – then watch them float away like bubbles.

Gives a whole new meaning to a
'bubble bath' doesn't it!

Finally, once you have stepped out of the bath, dry
yourself off with your hairdryer and as you do, imagine
that any remaining 'bubbles' are swiftly 'blasted' away
from you.

And you're done! Ready to face the world as YOU again.

CHAPTER THREE

YOU define your 'beauty'

If only I had a penny for everytime that a woman walks into my treatment room and tells me that she doesn't want *'those* eyebrows'.

I'd be a very rich woman. A very very rich woman.

I can totally understand why someone would say that, I mean you only have to look around the highstreet and you see caterpillars and slugs lurking *everywhere.*

But for me, being Helen Taylor, I prefer to do things more... ***naturally.***

There is no one size fits all when it comes to beauty, but there IS a size that 'feels like ME again', hence my Taylormade branding.

I believe that the only look that you should be working towards is the one that leaves you feeling like YOU again... *Not Kylie, not Kim, and definitely not Beyonce.*

Trying to look like another woman, is like wearing the completely wrong bra size. It may look great for the first five minutes, but pretty soon you'll be standing out for all the wrong reasons...., like there's something just doesn't quite 'fit you'.

Your best kept secret #3

Always, always opt for Taylormade: what I mean by that is learn to embrace your uniqueness and then go pedal to the metal to enhance that.

When you come for your consultation, I always address you as 'a whole person'. I can see both the outside *and* the inside of you.

They don't call us 'therapists for nothing' – one little improvement on the outside, can lead to a massive improvement on the inside.

I certainly do not take the power of my role lightly!

When somebody asks me what I do for a living, I often find that a tough one to answer.

I mean, there is a huge glaringly obvious difference, between 'I help people change their appearance' to 'I help people improve their appearance as a way to help them feel better on the inside'.

The treatments that I offer are like a form of therapy, that go way deeper than outer beauty.

The little tale of the 4am eyebrows...

One of my most memorable 'life changing' moments, for both myself and also my client, had to be when she came in for semi permanent eyebrows. I can remember when she very first walked into my clinic, she entered as a frail and insecure woman. Her shoulders were hunched and she held the demeanor of a person who REALLY wanted the world to not notice her.

The tragic part about it all, was that the way that she was presenting herself, made her anything but invisible! As the conversation unfolded, it soon became transparent, that this was a woman struggling... Almost driven to a nervous breakdown actually, and all because of ... Her **eyebrows.**

I honestly kid you not here, this woman would get up at 4 in the morning, in order to give herself time to draw on her eyebrows. She had lost herself in a world of obsessing... Obsessing over the 'perfectly drawn eyebrow'. Her work life was *heavily* affected by this as she would often be late for work each morning... and her health, both mentally and physically, was naturally also suffering.

I remember sitting back and just simply looking at this woman, and I knew in my soul that I had to help her. This wasn't just as simple as giving her 'her; eyebrows. It was about setting her free from the chains that bound her. It was about giving her extra time to just sleep until the morning...

It was about peace of mind and a piece of sanity. When that particular client, came back to see me for her top up six weeks after she first gained HER eyebrows, I met a completely different woman. The woman didn't just walk into the clinic, she positively strode in... shoulders back, head held high... she simply exuded a different energy. Her energy was powerful.

Stories like that are why I LOVE running my business. Because somewhere behind the frosted glass of my Clinic, nestled in the bosom of my treatment room, is a transformation taking place, on such a level that it is honestly MIND BLOWING.

There have been days where I have left the Clinic, unable to sleep at night from thinking about certain women...

Women who come in and share their innermost thoughts and feelings with me... Women who tell me their life story...

Women who confess that they worry that their husband is cheating on them, or that their best friend is the other woman.

Nine times out of ten their gut feeling is attempting to guide them, and when I do meet a woman who is hell bent on resisting the truth, I cannot stop myself from shining a big light on her...

I of course mean metaphorically, although to them I am sure it feels literal!

I want you to think about the ways in which YOU are perhaps avoiding the mirror. How do you really see yourself? Are you happy with who you are on the outside, but it's society who has you questioning things?

Do the issues that you have about your appearance, really truly matter to you?

If they *do*, if it's something that you want to do, for your eyes only, then by all means, come and see me. One thing that I love about the clients who come to work with me, is that they are independent and strong women.

They know that it's empowering to choose how you want to age these days. They also know that if they invest in any treatments, then it's for their own happiness only.

They understand that taking care of their appearance, is like keeping your car running. You wouldn't expect your car to just keep on going, without putting petrol, oil and water into it, now would you?

Your appearance is the same. If you want to go the distance, you need to keep up with the maintenance.

But keeping up with the maintenance can be 'subtle', it doesn't need to be a hassle. Keep things nice and toned everywhere and make sure that you skin is hydrated...

Little tweakments here and there keep the whole car running... and only you ever need know you've had them. **#justforme.**

Self reflection: What would you change?

If you could choose 2 areas that you'd like to work on (appearance) what would they be?

If possible I want you to carry out this exercise in front of a mirror. Look yourself in the eyes, and when you have chosen your areas, I then want you to have a little chat with yourself...

Ask yourself: Do you REALLY want to improve or enhance things for all of the RIGHT reasons. If the answer is no, then ask yourself what's going on for you. And if the answer is YES and you're motive is self empowerment, by all means *come and see me.*

#justforme...

Make notes **#justforyou** so that you can remember any moments of inspiration, a-ha's and breakthroughs that this chapter gave to you:

_____

_____

_____

_____

_____

_____

_____

_____

_____

_____

_____

A dollop of taylormade therapy

Stand at your bathroom mirror and take a long, hard look at yourself. Then, take your favourite cleanser and remove *every trace of makeup.*

As you do this, feel the contours of your face, the texture of your skin. Take a little moment to just 'feel' things. Feel the skin you are in – your natural state of beauty.

Then, again – take a look at yourself.

And that's all there is to it. Learn to look, to notice, to connect and to appreciate.

Because you my dear, are a Goddess.

CHAPTER FOUR

Ignore the competition

The main thing that I have had to learn to do in business, (and in life in general), is to *ignore the competition*.

Your best kept secret #4

Ignore the competition – aspire to be different! Who wants to live their life as some cheap designer knock off?

You see the thing about trends is this ladies: they come in like a tsunami and they often pass just as quickly. In life, and also in business, *I want to be remembered.* I don't want to be like a 90's popstar, famous for all of five minutes then in the second hand box at a car boot sale.

I want to be *revolutionary*, I want to be a leader.

I have built my reputation as being 'Helen Taylor' and 'if Helen isn't offering something then it really isn't worth doing." Clients travel far and wide to come to me because they value the treatments that I am performing, and they trust that it is I who will deliver results with them.

The lesson that I want YOU to take away from this, is that you will always be faced with competition. ***In life, in love and in business*...** And if you're going to keep letting that get to you then you're going to find yourself coming to a standstill.

It's like standing at broken traffic lights, waiting for the green light to flash at you.

There comes this life changing moment where you realise that nobody's coming to rescue you and you've simply got to make a run for it.

It's like there's never the right time to do something, you just have to take that leap and DO IT.

Otherwise, you'll be sitting on the start line waiting... and life unfortunately doesn't wait for you.

Which leads me to a question: 'Why is it that we fear competition anyway? And just what is it that's stopping you?' I mean... *really stopping you*.

Chances are, it's a fear of not being good enough' but what exactly does 'not good enough' mean to you?

Just whose measuring stick are you using to measure YOU? And why do you think that you're the one falling short here?

The only person who you need to compare yourself to, is the you who exists deep inside of you. The you who feels stifled, and the you who feels miserable.

I want you to think back to a time in your childhood when you were completely and utterly fearless.

I want you to take a moment now, to think back to the you in childhood. The you who didn't second guess herself, she just got up and boldly did things.

You didn't talk yourself out of things, and you wouldn't compare yourself to others. And if things on the off chance went 'wrong' for you, you showed your battle scars off in colour.

Whatever happened to that fearless girl? You know, she still exists inside of you.

Life changing moment: Look down and see that girl in front of you. Kneel down, and take her hands in your hands. Look her in the eye and say 'hello' to her. Reconnect with her... hug her. Tell her that you are sorry that she feels you've forgotten her... sorry for all of the times that you have ignored her.

Let her into your life again, and think about how you would treat HER.

We wouldn't ever dream of telling the little girl we once were that she is worthless, fat, old or ugly. We would never ever try and stop her from doing anything that she put her mind to.So why do we frequently treat ourselves like that?

'Believe in yourself, and all that you are – know that there is something inside you that is greater than any obstacle' –

Christian D Larson

I love this quote. When you believe in yourself on a deep, core level, the competition cannot even come close to you.

Being successful, whether in life, love or business, is about so much more than selling.

It's about knowing yourself on such a level, that the test of time simply cannot change you.

Sure, you may look a little different in your appearance, but the you who is at the core of you, remains constant throughout a lifetime.

When you truly connect to yourself on a deep, *really deep level*, nothing and nobody can *ever* compete with you.

Let me repeat that...

Nothing and nobody can *ever* compete with you...

The reason I am so sure of that? Because only YOU can share YOUR best kept secret.

Sure, others can try and copy you and to some extent, I guess that's a compliment.

But *nobody*, no matter how great a fake designer copy, can even come close to you being the original.

Self reflection: Market
the original

Here, I want you to think of yourself an original
designer handbag.

Okay, weird analogy, I get that.

But this can actually be really meaningful. What would
you be made of, what colour are you, what do you look
like and who would desire you?

Then I want you to think about how you would market YOU. Write a short description – go on, it's time to sell you! And what price tag would you put on YOU?

More often than not, us women are bloody marvelous at underpricing and undervaluing ourselves when we should be positioning ourselves like a Hermes handbag.

Hard to come by, often requiring a wait list and something to treasure for a lifetime!

#justforme...

Make notes **#justforyou** so that you can remember any moments of inspiration, a-ha's and breakthroughs that this chapter gave to you:

_____

_____

_____

_____

_____

_____

_____

_____

_____

_____

_____

A spritz of taylormade therapy

I want you to take your favourite perfume and then delicately spritz yourself. And as you do so, say to yourself, 'I am the original'.

Just like a signature scent, YOU are the original and nothing and nobody can compete with that.

They certainly cannot copy you.

And if they do? Well we all know what happens to 'knock off' perfumes... They wind up in the rubbish bin.

CHAPTER FIVE

Fall in love with ageing

Ageing...

Let's stop and talk about ageing for a moment.

Here's a question for you: 'How do YOU currently feel about ageing?'

Because I suppose, how you feel about ageing at say twenty... is very different to how you'd feel at 40...

At the time of writing this book I am currently in my early forties... and... I guess you could say that I feel sort of confused right now when I sit and think about *ageing*.

I know that that sounds a little...strange, for someone who works around people who are concerned with ageing.

You'd think that working in this industry, constantly up to date with the latest anti-ageing treatments, that I would feel ...okay with it.

But I guess that's a little like supposing that those who work in the funeral business, are totally okay with the thought of dying. The two don't always go hand in hand. And why should they? We are after all only human...

We all have that day when we face ourselves in the mirror, and somehow, something looks different.

It could be a slightly sagging jawline (go on, who here has ever stood there, pulling their skin right up towards their temple, wondering 'should I get a face lift?') or it could be those teeny tiny crows feet that suddenly resemble 'wrinkles'.

No matter what the details, of your first encounter with ageing, chances are, you feel rather let down by it.

I know that I did... but you know what? I sat back and thought to myself, that my early 40's was too 'young' to become obsessed about ageing.

Life is so short, isn't it? So I made an assertive and empowering decision to 'enhance' things.

Now, some people out there would say that the stronger choice would be to 'age gracefully' – but what exactly does that mean anyway?

Going back to that measuring stick – just WHO is it exactly who is out there, telling us what is appropriate behaviour when it comes to ageing... Or anything for that matter?

Nope, I decided that I just wanted to feel like me again – and that meant me a year ago, not me when I was in my twenties. It mean that I wanted to look a little less exhausted, and feel (+ look) refreshed again.

I know for a fact, working in my clinic, that most women don't want to look like their teenage self, and if you asked them 'what age they would like to look like', chances are they wouldn't know how to answer that.

Could you really answer that?

It's a tough one isn't it.

Your best kept secret #5

As you see yourself age on the outside,
you'll feel yourself age on the inside...
And this is not a bad thing.

#justforme – just for YOU. The only person's approval
that you ever need to get in life is your own. Period.

Self reflection: A look back at 'YOU'

You've seen people go wild over Throwback Thursday all over the internet haven't you? Well, I want you to do a throwback Thursday, even if today is not Thursday.

If it helps you to *dig out a photo,* then please by all means do so.

Next, I want you to remember who you were in that photo, at that age, and in that stage of life. What were your strong points and what were your 'weaker' points?

How did that YOU handle life? And how have things (and you) changed since then?

If you could give advice to the younger YOU, what is it that you'd say to her? Think about how much you've changed, and how you now handle life differently. Are you the you who you used to want to be? And if why not a) why not and b) what can you do to change that?

#justforme...

Make notes **#justforyou** so that you can remember any moments of inspiration, a-ha's and breakthroughs that this chapter gave to you:

_____

_____

_____

_____

_____

_____

_____

_____

_____

_____

A layer of taylormade therapy

I want you to grab your mascara and apply a coat of it. But not in the sophisticated way that you'd do it as a *lady*.I want you to think back to your younger self… perhaps when you were a teenager and apply it in the way that she used to.

Blast some of 'her' favourite music, and dance around as you do this. Look at how beautiful she is! She's still in there you know. A few wrinkles and some changes on the outside, really *cannot take away what's on the inside.*

Carry out this 'therapy' whenever you become lost in
the reflection before you.

Know that YOU have always been in there...
you just got lost amongst the rubble.

CHAPTER SIX

Fall in love with love

If there's one thing that's great for keeping us looking youthful... It's love.

That rosy glow, that wide eyed optimism. There's nothing like a great relationship to really get the blood racing again.

But love hasn't always been easy for me.

With two divorces under my belt, and several other breakups, I guess you could say that I have had to learn a LOT when it comes to romantic relationships.

Learn what, you ask me? Well – to smash down the walls that I had built around myself and to let someone close enough to love me.

Of course, sometimes, with some people, it felt like even when I did allow myself to do that, each time I let a man close to me, he'd either lie to me, hurt me or betray me... And the wall would come right back up again.

If I wanted to go deep and get really freudian here, I could probably pinpoint a lot of my 'issues' (if you have to call them that) back to my family.

But I'm not going to air my family's laundry here... That just wouldn't be ladylike! (But know that I am not in denial here.)

I have done my life coaching, I have been to counselling and I have *finally come to terms with things.*

In many ways, as I write this, I am actually in a balanced and happy place.

Between you and me, I think that I have *finally* found that time in life, where I personally feel more in control of things.

What's helped me reach such a place of inner peace? Well, I think that it's down to ageing. No... seriously. I honestly think, that as we get older, we a) gain more confidence, and b) stop tolerating drama.

But like I say... It's certainly not all hearts and flowers...

I can remember a time not that long ago when I found myself going through a breakup.

A breakup was nothing 'new' to me – but whereas perhaps with other breakups I had just ploughed on with things, this particular breakup *floored me.*

And it was through going through this breakup that I redefined what love meant to me. Let's stop and talk about that for a moment – love.
What does love mean to YOU?

'If you've found 'love' did it look like how you imagined it would when you were younger?'

You know... That your 'soul mate' would come charging up on a white horse to rescue you and you'd ride off into the sunset and live happily ever after?

Is that how love looks for you?

Chances are you're just like me and are smiling wryly with an 'of course not!'

Love, can come in all shapes and sizes, it can be with someone you never thought you'd end up with. Love can be heady and love can be wild. But love can also be BRUTAL. It can work its way inside of you and tear you up from the inside.

Love to me, is when you can still be standing together through it all...

There's an old saying out there somewhere, about how real love brings us face to face with the self who exists within us.

I hear so many clients (when we chat about relationships) say to me 'You know what Helen? I just want someone who will love me. The real ME' But when they go on to define who that real me is, they somehow don't seem to actually *like* her. Let alone love her.

Now I'm not saying that I am the epitome of personal development and have always truly loved myself. Come on, give me some credit here. But I have gone through some tough times and learned how to come through things and genuinely 'like myself'.

Isn't *that* a real achievement? What is all this pressure from 'self help gurus' who demand that we learn to love ourselves? Can't like be a happy medium? Isn't like more... realistic?

And some days, not really liking yourself can be a positive. If you've been a Diva to somebody, chances are today, you don't like yourself.

Life, just like love, is a cycle. A cycle of ups and downs, a cycle of positive and negative. And we need this cycle in order to maintain 'balance'. Nobody can be (or should try to be) happy twenty four seven.

And if you meet a person who oozes that, my advice is to run a mile from them. RUN!

#yourbestkeptsecret #6

Learning to like yourself means that you're already winning. So take some of the pressure off yourself and stop stressing about the whole 'self love' thing.

If YOU can learn to at least *like yourself*, then my darling, you're already winning.

Because it then doesn't matter what somebody else does to you. It doesn't matter if they want time out from you, and it doesn't matter if they end things.

If YOU like yourself as a person, you'll find a way to cope with things. You'll rise from the ashes with a smile, and throw on a whole heap of self value.

Of course, now... As I sit here and write this, I can confidently say that. But back then... Before I had risen from the ashes, I simply wasn't ready to move on.

Self reflection: Learn to 'like' yourself

If you had to write a list of things, that you actually like about yourself, what would be on it?

And you can guess what's coming next can't you?

Yes, go on... I want you to write this list, and I want you to then go and stand in front of your mirror and read this list out loud to yourself.

It might feel a little bit strange at first, but keep on doing it, and get louder and louder...

Feels good doesn't it? And if it doesn't that's something you need to work on. Practise, practise, practise, and *fake it 'til you make it!*

Just keep re-reading this chapter and take your time. I'm right here with you and *I'm not going anywhere. xxx*

#justforme...

Make notes **#justforyou** so that you can remember any moments of inspiration, a-ha's and breakthroughs that this chapter gave to you:

_____

_____

_____

_____

_____

_____

_____

_____

_____

_____

_____

A coat of taylormade therapy

I want you to find your boldest lipstick... Naturally RED springs to mind here, and I want you to draw on your bathroom mirror.

I know, I know, you're could well be thinking, 'But I only cleaned the mirror on Sunday!'. But let yourself go wild here, and draw on your bathroom mirror.

I want you to take your bright red lipstick (and if you don't own bright red lipstick, get your tush out there and buy one), and write 'I bloody LOVE myself!'.

Draw hearts, draw kisses. And then take that same red lipstick and add a coat to your lips. Look in that mirror and say it outloud – 'I bloody LIKE myself'.

CHAPTER SEVEN

Expect the unexpected

One big lesson that I have learned in life is that you never know what life has in store for you.

Expect the unexpected.

And that can work both ways – life is like a roller coaster, and just when everything is going great for you it can send you plummeting back down again. But on the flip side of that, life can also lift you higher than you ever imagined that it could, just as things seem bleak for you.

I have had times in my life (like we all have), where I have wondered if I would ever smile again.

The loss of my Dad being one of them...

And the really difficult breakup...

And during those times, I found it really difficult to just bounce back again. Have you ever had times like that? Where no matter how strong a person you are, it just feels like the middle has been torn out of you.

But one thing that has never ceased to amaze me, is how during those difficult times, life has had something in store for me.

A lesson...

A message...

A meaning...

#yourbestkeptsecret #7

Life will always turn the light off on you, but it's up to you when you turn it back on again.

Somehow, no matter how difficult and dark the journey was for me, life always handed me a glow stick. And with that glow stick, I was able to somehow start to see my way out of things ... It's like the Universe would always protect me.

This feeling... of always being protected, at the times when I really needed it, is what has given me faith, hope and optimism as I venture through this journey called life.

I wouldn't say that this is about religion. It's not even necessarily spiritual. It's about an unbreakable belief in the power within ME, that just knows, that even if I sink low... far lower than I could ever imagine, somehow I will always rise again.

It's this gut based, unshakeable belief in the power that exists within Helen.

I've also been fortunate enough, during those really dark times, to meet people that I like to call angels. You know the sort of person that I speak about – the kind who seem to appear out of nowhere... Who almost sense that you need to be reminded again... of the person who is hiding deep inside of you.

Have you ever met an earth angel? And do you still keep in touch with them?

Sometimes, these people appear out of nowhere, and may only be with you for five minutes. Literally. You may meet them on a train journey, or as you're sitting in a coffee shop.

It's like they just seem to know what to say to you, seem to know what you need to hear. And when they leave, you genuinely feel blessed to have met them. You just know that you met an angel.

Other people can come into your life, and remain in your life for a long time. They start out as angels, and then become friends, or even lovers. They touch you in such a way that you know that you'll never forget them.

During the 'breakup' that I shared with you, I met a certain angel.

I honestly attribute reaching a turning point to that particular meeting. Somehow I got in touch with myself again.

And that catalyst set me on the path that I needed to be on in order to make some changes.

It's the presence and the existence of these kinds of people, and the deep rooted belief in always coming face to face with myself again (no matter how hard life gets for me) – that keeps me feeling optimistic.

I know that even if I hit an obstacle, such a heartache, a loss, even health issues (I have recently had to face the menopause for example due to a hysterectomy), I will always do my best to look for the unexpected life lesson.

I will always, as long as I am breathing, do my best to turn any annoying negative into a really brilliant positive!

Take my menopause for example – I refused to allow the change in my life, hormones, moods, and overall health get the better of me. I created the Happy Hormone Company.

I like to see any negative period in my life as an opportunity to grow, and to find that golden needle in a rotting haystack.

When you can think of life a little like that, you never know what life will have in store for you.

Expect the unexpected...

In life, love, business, beauty and everything...

Everything is figure-out-able. No matter what is getting the better of you, there IS a way around it.

Self reflection: A look at your expectations

I want you to think about your expectations. Do you place unrealistic expectations on yourself? Have you forgotten how to let go of the reigns a little and enjoy the fluidity and magic of life?

What if you were to leave it in the hands of the Universe? What would you like it to deliver? Make a note of this in the #justforme section below.

Don't be afraid to let your mind run away with itself.The more passionate and descriptive that you can be ... the better!

Put it out there and then see what the Universe sends back to you.

#justforme...

Make notes **#justforyou** so that you can remember any moments of inspiration, a-ha's and breakthroughs that this chapter gave to you:

_____

_____

_____

_____

_____

_____

_____

_____

_____

_____

_____

_____

A hint of taylormade therapy

I want you to take all of your makeup off, and just look at yourself in the mirror. Remind yourself of all of the reasons as to why YOU are beautiful.

Now I am not just talking about outer beauty, so please, even if you have some crows feet, or a big spot on your nose, try and look beyond that.

But look at yourself in all of your rawness, as your most authentic self here... And remind yourself of how many times you've caught yourself when life feels like it's let go of you.

Remember just how STRONG you are, and then look at yourself and say ...

THANK YOU.

Yes, the Universe has always got you – but you've had your back for even longer.

CHAPTER EIGHT

When that voice within starts screaming...

Sometimes in life, when that inner voice starts screaming, it can be all too easy to stifle it.

It's particularly easy to ignore things when it comes to personal relationships.

Have YOU ever found yourself in a situation where the voice within told you that something wasn't quite right somewhere? And if so, how did you handle it?

Did you listen to the voice and act on things, or did you try and silence it?

The minute that you decide to silence it, is the minute that you turn your back on YOU.

There have been many times in my life where my inner voice started screaming, and I'd like to think that I was good hearing it – I've listened to what it was saying and made some really great decisions based upon that.

Had I not listened to that gut feeling, I might not be here today doing what I am doing and running this very business.

And then there have been times when listening to the voice within wasn't easy because I knew I would need to challenge some things.

Take that particular relationship.. When I went back to try and work through things, I just KNEW that something big was being kept from me.

Of course, being Helen Taylor there was only so long that I could go on like that, and unfortunately when my fears were proved to have weight to them, I was worried that I'd have to walk away...

However, this particular period proved to be a very important learning curve for me.

I realised that in this instance, I didn't WANT to walk away from things, and I was also at an age and stage in life where I didn't need to explain my choice to anyone.

Through raising the bar and redefining my standards, I was able to very clearly set my boundaries. And from that moment forwards, anyone who wanted a relationship with me would need to understand that I could and WOULD walk away from things.

#yourbestkeptsecret #8

Things can be as bad as you thought they were but they can be fixed and you can move on from it.

As a result of this experience, we were able to reach a place of understanding. I didn't try to control him (and I didn't actually want to...) – rather than focus on the relationship, I focused on working on *Helen*.

And I learned a very important lesson, in life, love and business – that although things may be as bad as you thought they were, they can be fixed and you CAN move on from it.

This time, rather than walk away I made a choice to stay and work through it...

And the rest as they say, is history.

I had learned a lesson in how to trust myself. And I knew that from this moment forward I would be just fine, if I listened to the voice within.

Self reflection: Learn to 'trust' yourself

How many times in YOUR life have you lost the ability to trust yourself? What I mean by that, is how many times have you stopped listening to your intuition? How many times have you drowned out that 'voice within'?

Have there been times where you had an experience like I had? Where that voice within you was SCREAMING?

It could have been to do with a relationship, or a friendship, or somebody that you met through your work environment. But somehow, somewhere inside of you you just KNEW that something wasn't 'right' somewhere.

Did you listen to that voice that was screaming? Or did you do what most of us are great at... did you silence her with comfort food, or attempt to drown with a bottle of Pinot?

If you could give one piece of advice to the person that you were when that happened, what would you say to her? Talk to her, or if it's easier, why not write her a letter?

Make peace with yourself, and *cut the cord to the past*. Then make a promise to yourself that if ever your inner voice speaks to you in the future you will listen to it *intently*.

#justforme...

Make notes **#justforyou** so that you can remember any moments of inspiration, a-ha's and breakthroughs that this chapter gave to you:

_____

_____

_____

_____

_____

_____

_____

_____

_____

_____

A splash of taylormade therapy

Have you ever found yourself wandering around the makeup counters in a department store, and wondered if you could pull off that lipstick?

Or perhaps it's a new shade of eyeshadow...

Do you always stick to the same old beauty products, almost afraid to try something different incase it doesn't suit you?

Well, today, I want you to go to that beauty counter, it can be in store or online (I know you may be busy), and I want you to browse the items a little and then when something 'jumps out at you' BUY IT.

Pick it up and buy it, or hit that button and BUY IT!

Listen to your gut feeling and see where it takes you.

CHAPTER NINE

Walk away with confidence

Walking away with confidence is a lesson that I had to learn in life. It's not easy to just walk away from things and you can spend a lifetime overthinking it.

So in this chapter, I want to talk a little bit about how and why I have often walked away (and not always felt great in doing that), and how you can, when necessary, walk away from things... **with confidence.**

#yourbestkeptsecret #9

Walking away from the wrong things makes a nice cosy space for the right things.

I am a great believer in being my most authentic self in order to attract everything that is meant for ME. The time that is spent chasing the wrong things only takes me further away from ME.

Sometimes of course, I may try and ignore this philosophy, because it can mean having to walk away from things... And sometimes, that can include certain people.

When I made the decision to walk away from both of my marriages, there was nothing 'easy' about it. Some people see walking away as being a cop out. Of course, if I had walked because I simply didn't want to work at it, I suppose then I might also agree with that.

But if something really isn't working for YOU and almost feels like it goes against the grain for YOU – then it takes a hell of a lot of strength and determination to be the one to end things.

Of course, there have also been times in my life, where I have found it much easier to end things. Not everything or everyone has a deep emotional attachment.

Sometimes letting go and walking away can be as simple as realising that 'actually I don't really care about this' – and in those instances, walking away can feel liberating.

But there have been times in my life, when I found myself in a situation with a client, where I have had to debate whether to cut ties and walk away from things.

Now I am not going to air the full details. I have more respect for the friendship that we had than that. But let's just say that when a friendship ran into troubled waters, and this friend also happened to be a client, I had a rather big challenge in front of me.

I could have simply glossed over all that happened...

But I didn't want to feel negative energy, especially not when it came to my Clinic.

I am very much a person who likes to work on her energy. I hold the belief that a person can only affect you if you are the one who allows it. I knew. On a really deep soul level, that I was left with no other option than to cut the ties on this occasion.

And so that is what I did...

And not only did I lose a client, I lost the friends that she had also referred to my business.

Now some people would say this was ludicrous. Why let money go to waste? Why not just block out my feelings, and see it as 'business'. But that has never been the way that I view things.

I put my heart and my soul into my business. It's my brand, my baby, my name attached to it. And if I am not injecting 'Helen Taylor' into every single corner of my workspace then I myself won't want to be there.

And so I let go of this situation. And it left me feeling uneasy. I found myself wondering if I had done the right thing...

I sat with myself one morning, and thought about it – what would be the worst that could happen if she did any of the things that I worried about? Even the most popular and successful people out there have to ruffle some feathers.

The answer was simple: People can only affect you if you don't stand by your decision. People can only get to you, if you don't believe in your actions. We have to learn to say NO in life...

And feeling uncomfortable and a little nervous about that, I guess is what keeps us human.

I don't like to just be a b*tch to people...

But saying NO is healthy. It goes back to setting clear boundaries. Think about it – if we try to keep everyone happy we leave little time for what WE want.

Which I guess is the root of the problem – us women are GREAT at feeling GUILTY about things. And saying NO is one of them. We believe that we have to keep everybody else happy, at the expense of how WE feel about things.

It's why you see women running around on empty. Cooking *everybody else's dinner before they eat their own meal. And I mean both literally and* spiritually.

We've been raised by generations, who believe that being a woman, means putting yourself at the back of the waiting line.

But knowing this, and identifying with it, still doesn't make it feel easier... when you choose that it's okay to say no to things, when you decide that it's time to walk away from things... On a deep subconscious level, we still feel that sense of guilt about it.

What should really matter, is how do you feel when you choose to walk away? The guilt aside, do you feel a sense of freedom? Does that inner voice, KNOW, that walking away is what's best for YOU?.

If the answer to that is YES YES YES – then the answer is to walk away from things.

Sometimes, there is no right decision even – sometimes, making an active choice not to change things and take a 'wait and see what happens' attitude can be incredibly moving.

It goes back to the belief that the Universe has bigger plans for you.

Sometimes, we just need to throw it back to the Universe and trust, that whoever, and whatever it truly right for us, will come and fill that empty space and sit with us. And that if we stop worrying,and pushing, and pulling – and just let things unfold ... one day the answer will become clear to us.

Going back to 'that' breakup...

I made a decision to stay and experience things – but that is different to choosing to work at it. I had simply increased my self worth, and knew that HE had to be the one to pursue ME.

If it was meant to work out then he'd come to me, and if it wasn't going to work... Then time would simply reveal that.

By NOT pushing and not pursuing, I freed up some of my energy. I allowed myself to focus on other things.

Of course, at times it was difficult. I still had nights where I just lay awake and thought about him. But I realised that when those niggling thoughts came I needed to learn how to question them. I would ask myself is this a real doubt? Is there any weight to it? OR, is it just my inner fear, attempting to take over?

More often than not I knew when I was simply 'worrying' about things and I allowed my mind to let go of it. I became very aware of my own headspace, and my desire to take control of it.

At the end of the day, aside from being in a relationship, I was also running a business. I couldn't allow my personal life to make such a dent in my work life. It all became about balance.

Ironically, as a result of this, I have been able to 'grow' from this process. As I said in a previous chapter, sometimes, even the hardest times, are sent to us for a reason.

Self reflection: How do YOU walk away from things?

I want you to sit down now and have a little talk with yourself. I want you to think of two things. The first is a time when you walked away from things… and the second is when you chose not to.

Next, ask yourself, how did you feel about your decision? How did it feel when you walked away from things and how did it feel when you chose not to?

Make a note of those feelings using the justforme journal section below.

Then, thank yourself – for having the strength and the courage to walk away from things. Not everyone learns how to do that. And if you feel that this is an area you'd like to develop strength in then now is the time to give yourself permission to do that!

#justforme...

Make notes **#justforyou** so that you can remember any moments of inspiration, a-ha's and breakthroughs that this chapter gave to you:

_____

_____

_____

_____

_____

_____

_____

_____

_____

_____

_____

A blast of taylormade therapy

Head to your bathroom, bedroom or wherever it is that you keep your beauty products and take a good old look at what's in there. Are you holding onto things, that simply are of no use to you?

If so, it's time for me to go Marie Kondo on you! Grab a bin liner and throw out anything that isn't used for you, doesn't suit you or doesn't appeal to you.

And DO NOT FEEL GUILTY about this! Don't overthink
things. Just pick the items up one by one, hold them,
and if it doesn't excite you – throw it in the bin bag!
Then dispose of it all... quickly.

You'll be surprised at how 'clear' you feel by doing
this – and you can also apply this to every room
in your home, not just your beauty cabinet. It's
amazing how much we 'hold onto' things,....
through surrounding yourself with the clutter,
you miss the things of any value.

And when do you finally rediscover them they've
usually expired.

CHAPTER TEN

How to live life confidently

In the last chapter I talked about walking away from things, in this chapter I want to focus on walking *into* things. Not literally of course, as that would just be painful!

I mean walking with confidence into a room, into a relationship, or into a business deal.

I mean learning the art of saying YES to things, as opposed to telling yourself no.

How many times in your life have you wanted to go up and talk to that person, apply for that dream job, but somehow talk yourself out of doing so? How many times have you decided that you're not smart enough, not pretty enough, not hot brave enough or not thin enough?

Going after what you want in life, can often present a challenge. It can really bring up the insecurities in you.

How many times have you lay awake at night worrying about what might happen if...

If things go wrong for you...

Or ... perhaps it's not about things going wrong for YOU... maybe you are someone who worries about things actually going RIGHT for you.

Whether it's a lack of self confidence or real fear based on past experience, putting ourselves out there and going after things is going to require confidence.

I can think of a few times in my own life, where I've wanted to walk (or run!) from things! Writing this book in a way, is one of them! Opening myself up within these pages leaves me... Vulnerable.

But I believe that in life, pushing through your fears empowers you.

#yourbestkeptsecret #10

In the words of Susan Jeffers 'Feel the fear and do it anyway'. Once you push through that fear, you'll feel like you're completely unstoppable.

It really is something that I find difficult to explain to you, because it's one of those things that you can only really 'get' when you go out there and do it.

I like to push myself and get out of my own comfort zone, on a fairly regular basis. I like to think of it a little like exercise. You don't WANT to go for that run at five in the morning but you know that if you do it, you're going to feel really GREAT afterwards.

The buzz... the adrenaline...

Going out of your comfort zone is a little like exercise for the soul isn't it. You need to make it your priority to give your soul a good work out, at least on a monthly basis.

Whether it be signing up for that night class, getting back on the dating scene, or finally booking that bungee jump! We all have 'something' that we want to do that scares us. Think about what you'd like to do and take a step towards doing it.

Lock it down, make it public – tell your social network about your plans to do it.

I can think of plenty of examples in my life, where I have made a choice to just do it – skiing is one great example. Just recently I pushed myself through my fears and did my first Black Run!

Of course, I was nervous, and of course a little voice in my head was telling me not to do it. But if you get the right mindset, you really CAN push through that.

And that's what it all comes down to isn't it. It all comes down to mindset. In life, in love, in business, in everything! Mindset is KEY in all aspects of living.

When I very first set up my business, I chose to have a positive mindset. As I said right at the beginning of this book, I have come a VERY long way since I started out on this journey – but it's 100% down to my mindset.

ACTION is also a must here, because you can have the most positive mindset but if you're not going to actually act on things, you run the risk of becoming a dreamer. Stop dreaming, and start doing – what do you have to lose here?

A-ha, but THAT is where the fear comes back into it, isn't it?

'What do you have to lose here' – let me ask you that very question... 'what DO you have to lose here?'

If you really, truly went for it, and did the thing that you want to do that scares you, what is the worst that could happen? Think about it... I mean really, really think about it. Write down all of the things that you fear, and then come up with a solution.

A solution? Yes. Write down a solution. So for example, if your biggest fear about going on that date, is that you're worried that the guy might not be attracted to you, ask yourself what would you do here?

Picture yourself in that very scenario, and break it down, gently. Bit by bit. Ask yourself, what does that REALLY feel like for you? If the guy just was not into you, why does the thought of that scare you? Usually, behind any kind of fear, you can link it back to a past experience.

Can you? And if you can, can you remember what THAT experience felt like for you? I have a friend who is a Hypnotherapist, and she taught me this great technique to move past that. Are you ready to try it out with me?

You are? Great, then let's get started. Find a space where you feel comfortable and where you're not going to be disturbed for a bit. Close your eyes, and imagine yourself at a time in your life where you experienced 'your fear'. If it was being rejected by another person, put yourself back there and 'feel' that.

If it was losing your money on a business deal... Put yourself back there and feel that.

Next, imagine yourself, standing right in the middle of that scenario and give the way that you are feeling a colour. For example, you may be feeling anxious and would describe that anxiety as a purple. Or you may be feeling angry and describe it as a red. Let yourself really feel it, and then let yourself choose a second colour – one that makes you feel POWERFUL... Allow that colour to become the dominant one as it works its way through you.

Notice how fast your energy changes. Next, whilst you are feeling really energised, allow the background around you to fade now... Watch it as it turns to black and white, and fades smaller into the distance.

Then, open your eyes. Feel your feet planted firmly into the ground beneath you. Shoulders back, stand tall and proud and confident. Know, that YOU have the power within you, to change your headspace and your physical state in just a matter of minutes.

Safe in the knowledge that you can do this, know, that from this moment onwards, whenever you find yourself questioning things, or whenever you find yourself anxious – you can carry out this simple exercise and change the way that you feel.

In changing the way that you feel, you disempower the negative mindset and make a choice to step back and change it. Sometimes, we can get carried away with the voices that guide us – it's so easy isn't it to allow fear and worry to take over.

But knowing that you can change the way that you feel about things, puts you back in the driver's seat.

If you can stop your anxiety and fear from engulfing you, you can make a clear choice to just go for things: Because you can handle the thing that is stopping you.

Sure, that guy might not like you, you may lose some money, you may fall on your bum and have to get up again – but unless it's a life or death situation, you really WILL be able to handle things.

In knowing how to work through your fear, you can then go after what you want in life.

Self reflection: Write a brand new bucket list

Did you ever write a bucket list? If not, you're about to. It's a great way to set give yourself a reminder of all of the things you'd like to do in life.

It may be that you want to do them before you turn 40, or 50, or 60... set yourself a time limit.

Or, it may just be a general list, where you add to the list weekly, monthly or annually.

Print the list off and keep it in places where you can see it. And each time that you achieve something on that bucket list, make sure that you celebrate. Reward yourself by taking that weekend to Paris, or buying that brand new handbag. It never hurts to have a little motivation.

#justforme...

Make notes **#justforyou** so that you can remember any moments of inspiration, a-ha's and breakthroughs that this chapter gave to you:

_____

_____

_____

_____

_____

_____

_____

_____

_____

_____

_____

_____

A stroke of taylormade therapy

For this little exercise I want you to go and buy a body brush, one of those with the really long handle. Then, next time that you are in the shower, I want you to enjoy some body brushing.

Body brushing is great for stimulating the lymphatic system and helping to remove any toxins. I recommend that you always brush towards you heart, which is great for circulation and dry body brushing is most effective.

As you begin your brushing, imagine that with every brush stroke you are brushing away your mental toxins, and all of those negative thoughts that are stopping you. And with every brush stroke, try and repeat this mantra:

'I give myself permission to let go of you' – say this for every thought that you desire to leave you.

CHAPTER ELEVEN

How to take action quickly

"I am so pleased with Helen's work.
My only regret is that I didn't do it sooner"

Katie, a client.

Have you ever heard the saying that the
Universe responds to speed?

Well, if you haven't I am here to introduce you
to that very concept.

*The Universe loves speed – which means that the faster
that you choose to do something, the better the chances
that you're going to succeed at it.*

I have always adopted this principle, in my life and also my business. When I want to do something I simply make it happen.

Take this book for example, when I decided that I wanted to write it, I gave myself a deadline of ... Oooh a month from when I first sat down with the concept.

I need to work with speed on things, otherwise I start to talk myself out of things...

'What on earth are you even thinking about Helen?'

'What makes YOU think that you can do this?'

It's flipping annoying let me tell you – and if you're anything like me, you yourself have been there. You feel all excited and confident one minute, and then the next you're talking yourself out of it.

Take the quote at the start of this chapter from my client, Katie.

Katie feared that things would go wrong for her. However, she was thrilled with the end results (and her eyebrows) and in her own words, she said, 'she just wished she had done it sooner!'.

Of course, fear, anxiety and worry, are all a normal part of daily living. It's NORMAL to worry about things going wrong for you – but it's when the fear and worry takes over that you need to address your mindset.

Yes fear is perfectly normal but it's how you choose to act on it that makes the biggest difference. Fear, if left to run riot can lead to self sabotaging behaviour – for which I have a zero tolerance policy.

But it takes a lot of practice to become good at that. I have spent many a night awake worrying, wondering and driving myself crazy with over analysing...

Should I be doing this...

Should I be doing that?

And of course this is perfectly normal. But being the competitive person that I am in life (and always have been since being little), it takes a hell of a lot to stop me, from doing what I want, in life, love and business...

I am a 'go girl, and make it happen' kind of woman. I like to put my all into things and then celebrate any achievement.

In some ways you could say that I'm a perfectionist. But there's always been something about that word that I associate with being ruthless. Or dare I even say it... heartless.

I don't expect to be perfect. The battle that I fight is between me and myself only. I like to set myself a goal and then smash through it. I like to go above and beyond the ordinary.

In some ways I could attribute some thanks towards my Mother. It was her expecting so little from me that made me want to excel that. I suppose you could say that it was always made clear that more was expected from my brother.

I stopped expecting praise for things. Unless it was of course from my Father. His praise meant more to me than anybodies. But I decided that I had nothing to prove to anyone – I simply wanted to live my life MY way. That to me means success.

And the older that I get, the more competitive with myself I am becoming. I love this quote from CS Lewis:

"You are never too old to set a new goal or dream a new dream"

CS Lewis

Age doesn't seem to stop me. I simply see ageing as meaning that I am getting closer to the 'end' of things. The more that I hear that clock tick... ticking – the more that I think about all of the things that I still want to achieve in life.

And trust me – there are a LOT of them!

Which almost makes me want to rush through them! I honestly have this secret fear (I guess it's not so secret now that I'm sharing it with YOU), that if I were to leave this life NOT having done them all, then somehow THEN I would have failed at things.

I believe in pushing myself to excel. I currently have a Business Coach, and the most amazing team of people surrounding me, who help me hit goals in my Clinic.

I do accept that I cannot do *everything*. I make sure that my time and my energy is spent doing the things that I am best at.

So if for instance, I need to do some video editing, then I hire the very best editor. I don't waste time trying to do everything, and I have become a pro at outsourcing.

This means that I get to spend more time in my clinic, working with my fabulous clients, or sitting down in a meeting with my branding expert, looking at how to develop my business.

I always have a million and one ideas, racing around in this head of mine. It therefore makes absolute sense that I like to work my way through things. I live my life like it's one big bucket list. I love to write down all of the things that I want to achieve in life, and then sit and tick those things off that list. I am constantly hungry for the next thing.

#yourbestkeptsecret #11

The sooner you get started, the sooner things will be revealed to you.

Sometimes, if you sit and wait to see the 'whole' picture, before making a move and going for things – you'll find yourself sitting, waiting doing nothing.

You cannot expect to see the Ocean if you you're sitting chained up in the harbour.

But as soon as you set sail you'll discover that there's a whole world of 'good stuff' waiting for you. Once you let yourself run with it, the Universe will reveal all that it has in store for you.

Self reflection: Do you need to spring into action?

If you look back at your life and are truly honest – are you the person who grabs hold of things, or do you find yourself sitting on the sideline?

It could be that you're quite happy sitting on the side line – I do get that we are all individual and 'different'.

But, I think it's safe to say that for most of us, we'd like to spring into action and make the most of what life has in store for us.

Make a note using the #justforme journal and explore WHY you think that it is, that you find it hard to move quickly with things. Is it because of fear, or a past experience?

And how would life look (and feel) for you if you were to wake up tomorrow to something different?

#justforme...

Make notes **#justforyou** so that you can remember any moments of inspiration, a-ha's and breakthroughs that this chapter gave to you:

_____

_____

_____

_____

_____

_____

_____

_____

_____

_____

A hint of taylormade therapy

Have you ever turned to the power of aromatherapy as a way to create the right mood for things?

Lavender for example is said to be calming and balancing, where as lemongrass is said to be energizing.Today, I want you to enjoy a little shopping spree, and go and explore the world of essential oils.The goal of this exercise is that you discover a scent that works for YOU and you use it as a way to change your mood state.

If for example you feel that you are putting off doing something that you want to do but you know that FEAR is getting the better of you, then turn to Lavender in order to calm things.

OR, if you are generally feeling exhausted, what with work, kids and family and you need to find the energy with which to do things, it might be time to pull out the lemongrass.

You can use essential oils either in their pure undiluted state, for example, in an oil burner... Or why not treat yourself to a naturally scented candle? Body lotions, and even massage oils can also work well for ths... As can those rollerball oils that you pop on your wrists and temples.

CHAPTER TWELVE

How to make friends with your fear

Fear... Ahhh...

Is fear my friend or enemy?

In the last chapter I talked about walking into things...
Opportunities, relationships, business ventures,
adventures... I talked about putting **YOU** out there, and
pushing through your fear.

After a nights sleep and some reflection, I have had a little think about that, and whilst I stand by every word that I say there, I also don't want you to think that I am not friends with fear.

Talking about knowing how to 'feel the fear and do it anyway' and how to push through my fear, may give you the impression that fear rarely gets the better of me. But this is simply not true.

I wanted to expand on the concept of fear, because my relationship with it is quite complex. And so in this chapter, I want to open up more about fear – about MY fears, and how (and when) I deal with them...

Fear isn't something to be stifled. Fear comes up as a way for our subconscious mind to talk to us. Fear communicates.

And so from that, the first thing that I want to say about fear, is that it's important that you HEAR IT.

Listen.

Really listen to your fear.

And that doesn't mean listen and then go into panic mode and self sabotage things (hands up who else is great at doing that?). It means sit back, listen, and then take a step back and just be aware of the presence of your fear.

Sometimes, fear rears its head to protect us – our subconscious mind knows that once upon a time in our history, a similar situation happened and the outcome wasn't great for us. It therefore attempts to protect us by sending in the 'ready for battle' kind of fear.

The fear who shows up at two in the morning, wakes you forcefully from your slumber and tells you it's time to protect things.

Other times, fear shows up because deep down you are perhaps excited... There may be some BIG change that lies ahead of you, and despite knowing that this is good for you, your subconscious attempts to resist it.

Why? Why does it do that? Does your subconscious mind hate you? Because it sure as hell can sometimes feel like that, can't it? But nope. Your subconscious doesn't hate you., It just wants to do right by you. It wants to keep you safe from anything that may pose risk to you.

And what YOU see as risk, and what your subconscious mind sees as risk, can be two different things altogether.

What's important here, is to be really brutally HONEST with yourself. Take a deep look at your fear, and ask yourself what could be going on here. Because sometimes, sure, we need to LISTEN to our fear, especially if it's trying to protect us...

BUT if your fear is repeating a pattern, and you know that you don't want it to get the better of you then it's up to YOU to refuse to allow it to do that.

Which means, having the unshakeable belief in what it is that you're striving for.

If for example, it's a huge business deal, and you feel really out of your depth – sit with your fear and ask yourself, how would you feel if you ran away from things?

Would you be okay with that or would it be the wrong move for you?

Listen to what your fear is trying to tell you and then make a decision based around that. Sometimes, your fear is screaming at you because it has a very valid reason to. In which case, ask yourself why is it that you keep refusing to hear it?

Because it may be that actually, what you need to do this time, is listen to your fear and look at what it's throwing up for you.

For me, fear is usually (but not exclusively) associated with change.

At the time of writing this book, I am going through some BIG changes – I am redefining my entire brand philosophy. I am about to launch a product line, and I am of course trying to get this book finished.

There have been several moments, where I have woken at the witching hour, riddled with self doubt and fear. There have been numerous phone calls to my business coach and the team around me, just checking that I am on the right track here.

And the most ludicrous part of all of this, is that I KNOW that I am on the right track ...I just am scared about the changes in front of me.

I am scared for example that redefining my brands message may not sit right with some clients...

I know that in this very exciting journey, I may lose some friends along the way. That of course upsets me. But I also have to stand by my core belief system, which is that when you come from a place of authenticity, the people, the things, the experiences, the opportunities... All of the things that are RIGHT for YOU will suddenly find their way to you.

But sure, this process has not been 'easy'.

That's what I mean when I say just trust in the process, feel the array of feelings, and know, that as long as you listen to your fear, but don't allow it to just control you – then that is where the magic happens.

See fear as a learning process. See it as being something that pops up to challenge you. See it as that friend who means well, but can be ever so slightly annoying, when they arrive and attempt to confront you.

Sometimes, you'll end up saying 'do you know what, I think you're right here' OR you'll have to stand your ground with them and say 'I know you mean well and I love you, but I'm going to go ahead and do MY thing here'.

Sure, it won't feel comfortable, and you'll question yourself over and over. But you'll end up where YOU are meant to be. As long as you listen to what the voice within is telling you, you will always end up where you are supposed to be.

#yourbestkeptsecret #12

Think of fear a little like Angel/Devil that sits on your shoulder. Sometimes it has good intentions, and other times its out to destroy you. Always keep your wits about you, and choose to listen to the sound of YOUR voice, because that always outshines fear.

I like to see fear as being here to test me.

And so as I go through this whole process, each time that I write about something and ask myself 'should I be saying that?' I like to remember that as long as I am being true to myself, and as long as I believe in that moment, that I am on the right path, then everything is exactly as it should be.

You see, in this thing called life, we cannot predict the future. We can only ever do what we FEEL is best, at any given moment. And the choices that we made yesterday may not be the choices that we'll make tomorrow.

Life is fluid and things are forever changing.

Us, as people are just like the seasons. The you who you are at twenty is nothing like the you who you are at forty. Therefore, the choices that you made as a teenager, might not be the choices that you'd make in your forties, but they WERE the right choices for the you who you were as a youngster.

I guess what I am trying to say here, is that you can't allow fear of *'what if'* to take over.

You could spend all day and night over analysing things. But if you get too caught up in that process, you miss the moment and the magic that surrounds you.

All you can do is your best (and what feels right) in this moment, and that is all that anybody (and yourself) can ask of you.

Self reflection: Make friends with your fears.

Sit down in a place where you feel safe and comfortable and look back at your life for a moment. Ask yourself, how many times have you let fear get the better of you. Then, ask yourself, was that decision justified? Was fear out to get you or was it trying to protect you?

Then, forgive yourself. Just let it go – all of the times when you self sabotaged things or let that fear control you. Know, that you did what you felt was right for YOU in that moment and that itself was what was right for you.

Then, make a pact with yourself to make friends with your present and future fears. Allow yourself to sit down with them, grab a coffee, and be open to simply listening to them, KNOW that YOU are the one in control of things, but make a space for fear to sit with you.

How do you feel in this moment? Doesn't seem so scary right now, does it.

#justforme...

Make notes **#justforyou** so that you can remember any moments of inspiration, a-ha's and breakthroughs that this chapter gave to you:

_____

_____

_____

_____

_____

_____

_____

_____

_____

_____

_____

A smidgen of taylormade therapy

Next time that you are applying your night cream I
want you to take just a smidgen of it and as you apply
it, talk gently to yourself, and remind yourself, that no
matter how much fear tries to wake you, you're going
to sleep peacefully tonight. YOU are in control of things
and it's you who is in the driver's seat.

You are all too aware of fears presence, and you know that sometimes it can be good for you. But you are also aware that on the majority of occasions, fear is out to get you. Remind yourself of this, and allow yourself, as and when fear arises, to simply allow it to wash over you. You do not need to listen to it, it will still be there in the morning.

Then take a look at yourself in the mirror, and give yourself permission to just *let go go things*. It'll all be there in the morning.

CHAPTER THIRTEEN

How to learn to just trust in things...

Trust... it's a funny old thing isn't it? Learning to trust and issues with trust, is a subject that often pops up at the Clinic, especially when I am treating my clients.

If you think about it, just the very act of coming for a treatment involves an element of trust – trust that I will help you look (and feel) like 'YOU' again, and trust that you can confide in me.

It never ceases to amaze me, just how much my clients open up to me and I am really, truly honoured by that.

I can remember one time when one client, was lay on the couch having her eyebrows done. She told me about her boyfriend, and how she felt that he MUST be cheating... She'd often had to deal with her own 'trust issues' so when her gut was desperately reaching out to her, she wasn't sure whether to listen to it.

'He has to be cheating' she said 'I just FEEL it'.

I can remember asking her what she planned to do about it. Then suddenly her whole tone changed. 'Well I don't have any proof yet do i... I don't think that I can do anything. I mean... I am not even SURE whether he is actually cheating on me so....'

It was in that moment that I looked at her and said 'do you think it's your fear that's talking here, or do you actually FEEL that he's cheating?'. I asked her that because she had often had fears and worries about losing him, that weren't actually based on anything concrete.

'I can't put my finger on it' she said ... 'I just feel that something isn't right here'.

Have you ever had times when you have felt like that?
Like you can't even put your finger on it, but you just
KNOW that something isn't right somewhere. If so, how
did YOU act on it?

DID you act on it? Or did you choose to do nothing?
And what exactly was the outcome?

You see, learning to trust the voice within is something
that many of us struggle with. It's like we need solid
proof to act on things... when sometimes, the very fact
that our voice within is not happy, should be more than
enough for us to listen to.

It goes back to being your most authentic self doesn't
it, When you are YOU and are completely in tune with
YOU – then anything or anyone that doesn't sit right
with that, in the long term must not be right for you.
And you do not need to feel guilty about that.

Let me repeat that...

You do NOT need to feel guilty.

I don't know about you, but I think that sometimes, us women are great at feeling guilty when we step up and say no to things. Or in the case of trust, if we voice and challenge things.

It's almost as if we are saying 'I am listening to my intuition here – but I am still not sure whether to follow it'.... I am still not sure whether to *trust* in it. And when it comes to trust, I think that the biggest journey that you'll have in life,, is about the level on which you trust yourself.

Yes, it's great to sit with your best friend and chat over a coffee, it's good for the soul to let it all out and ask someone's advice. But the way that they see things, the way that they would handle things – that's their inner voice speaking and what their inner voice may choose to do, will be entirely different to yours.

It takes a lot of courage, and dare I say, ageing, for us to become comfortable with trusting our own choices. We live in a culture where we turn to friends, magazines and life coaches for advice...

But at the end of the day, the only person who you have to be answerable to,

is YOU.

#yourbestkeptsecret #13

When you trust the voice within, it doesn't matter what goes on around you. You can walk confidently through your life knowing that every step that you take is the right one for you.

How many times in your life have you put off grabbing that opportunity, because somebody whose approval meant a lot to you, didn't quite approve of things? Or, how many times have you followed a path that you just knew wasn't entirely right for you, and then found yourself regretting it?

I know that there have been many occasions in MY life, where I have said to myself 'If only I had just listened to myself'... Or something along the lines of, 'I just KNEW that there wasn't something right with that/them'.

Learning to trust yourself is firmly connected to the whole intuition thing. It's all very well and good to hear your intuition guiding you. But if you then step back and question things, it's easy to become distracted.

Especially when it comes to asking the advice of others – now don't get me wrong, asking advice on things is brilliant – I love when a client asks me how she should handle things... Whether it's to do with a relationship, a career move or a friendship, I believe that when women put their heads together over a problem, the results can be really outstanding!

But the one thing that I always say to them, is 'what do YOU think' or 'what do YOU want to do' ... it doesn't matter what your friend/mum/sister/therapist says. It's YOU who's advice you need to listen to.

Self reflection: Learn to trust in yourself

Make a list of all of the times in your life where you've had issues with simply **trusting things...**

Ask yourself, what is it that you have a hard time trusting?

Maybe it's another person, or maybe it's about trusting in yourself again. Make some notes in the #justforme journal and then sit back and have a chat with yourself.

Can you see a pattern? Or perhaps you've been through something really BIG in life, that's affected your ability to trust in things?

Maybe now is the time to speak to a therapist, or sign up to work with a life coach.

Give yourself permission to trust in things, and if nothing else, trust in YOURSELF again, Because no matter what else goes on around you, you are the one who can handle it.

#justforme...

Make notes **#justforyou** so that you can remember any moments of inspiration, a-ha's and breakthroughs that this chapter gave to you:

_____

_____

_____

_____

_____

_____

_____

_____

_____

_____

A layer of taylormade therapy

When you've had a bath or shower, take some luxurious body cream and massage it into your shoulders.

Next, I want you to gently massage your neck and as your arrive at your throat area, gently place your hands over it and say 'I trust the power of my voice within'.

Repeat this exercise daily if you want to, and adapt it to when applying your day cream and night cream.

Really take care of your throat chakra, and appreciate the voice that you have right now. It doesn't matter if yesterday it fell silent on you. Today you have a chance to change that.

CHAPTER FOURTEEN

How to get back to reality

I don't know about you, but sometimes, I sit back and look at life and it all seems a bit... Hectic.

Running a business, maintaining a social life, some days it can feel like finding time for some 'me' time is like trying to achieve the impossible.

We live in a world where women are expected to have their cake and then some... Gone are the days where a woman was expected to learn how to bake the perfect sponge cake whilst looking after the children.

Today we are expected to run our own business, be a domestic goddess, a diva in the bedroom, and play the perfect hostess.

I personally do not have any children – but I saw a fab quote on Facebook that said something along the lines of 'we expect women to raise their children like they don't work, and work like they don't have children'.

And I think that sort of sums things up perfectly.

Whether you choose to have children or not is your business. Whether you choose to work or not is your business. Whether you choose to make a lot of money or not ... Your business.

You my dear are answerable to no-one.

The only person that you need to answer to is YOU – are you living the life that YOU want to be living?

Because true happiness, and real success... Well that comes from being in the life that YOU want to be in. Not the one that society says you should be living, not the one that your parents think you should be living and not the one that the media thinks you should be living.

We live under (and put ourselves under)
SO much pressure.

It's not helped by the fact that we live in an age where we are slaves to social media. Facebook, Instagram and Twitter... What originally started as a social thing has now taken over our lives completely.

I get a great deal of my business through Facebook... Don't get me wrong, I am not objecting to it...

But...

Turning off my smartphone and detaching from virtual reality can feel like losing a limb sometimes. We would all like to do a bit more of that (turning the phone off that is. Not losing a limb), so why does it feel so ... *difficult?*

And then there's the issue of how we appear on Facebook ... Working in the world of aesthetics has given me a real insight into the madness that it's instilling into women.

Women actually want to look like they do on social media – we live in a world where everything goes through a filter. And if we do not look like how we look on the internet, it can affect how we feel about going out in public.

I've read articles about women who are concerned that if they meet someone off a dating site, they will be rejected for not looking like who they do in their profile photo! It's complete and utter madness isn't it?

And the craziest thing about all of this, is that most of us feel the same way about this... we wish that we could step off the hamster wheel, wash off that makeup, post a makeup free selfie, and say 'this is the real ME, so deal with that!'.

So...

What's stopping you?

Would you ever do that?

And if not, why not?

Why is it that we have found ourselves comparing and competing? And we all do it. We do. On some, teeny, tiny level. And yes, to some extent, that's human nature. It's no different to when we were teenagers back in the playground, or in our twenties at the local wine bar.

Wine bar? Showing your age there Helen!

But you know what I am saying...

Even those of us who once said that we would not get sucked into social media... would not allow a virtual world to coincide with our real one. Where exactly do we draw the line between virtual and reality? Because today, the internet IS real.

We are living in a time where 'Keeping up with the Kardashians' is a form of 'reality' and we are happy to sit and peer into the lives of others.

We are a generation of voyeurs...

But where exactly do we draw the line with this?

How do YOU find time to unplug for a bit?

When and where do YOU draw your line in the sand when it comes to virtual reality? How do you step off the hamster wheel and just feel like YOU again?

It's important, that somehow, somewhere, we step up and reclaim *reality*. Otherwise the next generation will grow up thinking that real life is a life spent on Facebook.

Going back to aesthetics... Did you know, that one of the current issues when it comes to appearance, is that women feel that they are getting a 'turkey neck' much faster than say their Mothers used to?

Experts say that all of the time that we spend looking down at our smartphone is affecting not only our social skills and our posture, but is also having a negative impact on our appearance! *Radiofrequency* and *High Intensity Focused Ultrasound* are often requested at the clinic as a way to tackle that.

And then there's this whole 'fear of missing out' syndrome that the media often talks about – apparently we are hooked to our screens and the internet, because we are scared of missing out on things.

There was once a time when *fear of missing out on things* meant not being at that party, or not being out on the high street. The irony, oh the irony, of watching a society, who are scared of that, spending the best part of their existence, walking around glued to the internet, whilst completely missing out on the people, the natural beauty and the entire world in front of them!

I personally have had to make time in my busy schedule to detach from the madness and reconnect to ME again.

I make sure that once a week I do a virtual detox (which I will share with you shortly), and that I spend time just getting out in nature, walking the dogs, perhaps just sitting outside a cafe, just watching the world go by, watching life... *happening.*

Do you make sure that you unplug and make time for you on a regular basis? And if not, why not? Are you scared of missing out? Do you worry what other people will think of you?

Have YOU ever had to explain to somebody, why you didn't reply to their message on Whatsapp, because you were taking some time to just feel like you again? We live in a time, where people think that it's perfectly acceptable that we are all instantly contactable, 24-7, and if you aren't instantly contactable then there's got to be something wrong with you...

'Has she fallen out with me?'

'Did I say something to upset her?'

It's time we voiced up and found a happy medium. Reclaim your personal power and set your boundaries so you can connect to YOU again. And what better place to start with that, than a social media detox?

Here are my

back

- Make a decis
  you will sim

- Let those
  about thi

Then, go out into th
whatever makes yo
coffee. Go for

- If you feel that people ...
  about you, post a status on facebook.

- Make good use of the autoresponder, or
  chat bot and set one up on your email
  address, or your business page on
  Facebook. Let the virtual world do the
  talking for you. Thanks for your message
  but I'm currently not available.

e world and just do things. Do
u feel alive again ... go and get that
a walk. Take a class in how to make
scented candles.

Learn a foreign language...

Or figure out how to make cookies...

Take up knitting sweaters...

Just for God's sake do something different...

GO COMPLETELY OUTSIDE OF YOUR COMFORT ZONE.
GO RIGHT BACK TO THAT BUCKET LIST.

Think about all of the time that you spend scrolling.
Heck we don't even refer to it as surfing anymore, and
that sounded way much more... adventurous.

Now we spend our free time just scrolling...

Scrolling...

Scrolling...

Scrolling...

Tell me, aren't just sick of it?

Public announcement.. There will be no further chapters, I do not wish to write about life anymore, I am going back out there to live it!

No. No, I am of course joking.

Sort of...

#yourbestkeptsecret #14

Life is constantly happening, but only YOU can go out there and live it.

Forget what other people think of you. Just go right back to your roots again, If this means taking more time to listen to music then grab your headphones and do that. If you used to enjoy going camping and going for walks in nature, then please, whatever you do, DO THAT.

You only get one life – so live it.

And that is where I will end this chapter as I want you to go out and do things!

Self reflection: How much of your time is screen time?

This week, try and keep a track of your 'screen time'.

Look realistically at that end of the week figure, and ask yourself, is this something that sits okay with you? Maybe it is... maybe you're actually spending less time browsing the internet than you initially thought possible.

OR, perhaps the amount of time you spend online shocks you. Look at that figure again... Whether it's 2.5

hours or 12.5 hours... Just gently remind yourself that that is time that you will never get returned to you.

How else could you have spent those hours? Let's try and put things into perspective here: You could use those 2.5 hours to write a chapter of a book each week. OR, you could use those 2.5 hours to travel down to the seaside.

I know... I know! It's kind of crazy when you stop and think about it.

We spend so much time just mindlessly scrolling yet we claim that we don't have time to do other things... Like pick up that Vac and start cleaning... Or finally meet that old friend for that coffee...

Use the #justforme journal pages to keep a log of your weekly screen time and then add it up monthly. Ask yourself if you had that time as FREE time, how would you plan to spend it?

You'd head on down to the sea you say? Then please (no seriously) do send me a postcard!

#justforme...

Make notes **#justforyou** so that you can remember any moments of inspiration, a-ha's and breakthroughs that this chapter gave to you:

_____

_____

_____

_____

_____

_____

_____

_____

_____

_____

A shot of taylormade therapy

Next time you are in the bathroom and you are going to cleanse your face before bed, take a shot of cleansing lotion and remove your makeup vigorously.

Imagine the cleansing lotion lifting away all of the pollution and harmful rays from your skin – that it has absorbed from both the environment and also your screen time.

Remove that with warm water, followed by a splash of cold water and make a choice to have a bare faced detox from social media.

And breathe! Feels good doesn't it?

CHAPTER FIFTEEN

Face the future with *firm* determination

Now that you have had a chance to think back over things... about life and love and everything... It's time to think a bit about the future.

The future...

It can be a place and time that we are yet to find ourselves in, yet somehow it's presence already controls us...

The worry and anxiety that you have over the future, can totally define this very moment.

What would YOUR future look like, if you didn't worry about the things that might, just might *possibly* happen... things that might not *ever* happen!

Imagine, if you could click your fingers and have exactly the kind of future that you dream of...

What would that future look like? What kind of person would you be? Where would you live? And what would you be doing? Does your ideal future look anything like the life that you are *currently* living?

If not, ask yourself why not... And how *exactly* are you going to change things?

#yourbestkeptsecret #15

When you choose to face the future, with firm determination, everything you dream about suddenly comes into alignment with you.

You see, you are the creator of your own life story. You can start each day as a new chapter, and you can end each day by playing the role of the editor. If something doesn't sit right with you, then make a choice to change it!

You can always rewrite the ending, and take the role of director.

Life hasn't always gone the way that I would have planned it – there have been times, where I have been at my absolute lowest, and I wondered if I would ever feel like 'me' again.

But somehow, for some reason, I have always been able to reconnect to the Helen within, and find a way to shine a light on things. It doesn't matter how dark the day may become, I simply turn that light up brighter...

I've come to accept, through my four decades on this planet, that life is going to continually 'test' us. I used to believe that we should be striving to reach a destination ... a place of 'happiness'.

But now I realise that life isn't like that. And I am not so sure about the word 'happy'. I think that finding a place where I am feeling in check with myself, and in balance, is the closest thing to 'happiness'.

And I can bring myself into that space of balance (happiness) even when things aren't going 'right' for me. I think THAT is happiness... Being able to maintain a sense of self, even when it feels like the odds are against you.

I've gone through loss, heartache, and misery... But I don't regret one single moment of that. Because it's been the fuel to push harder in my business, and hey, I've managed to even write a book about it!

And as a I draw to the close of this book, I am excited about the next installment that life has in store for me... because this book shall not 'define' me. This is a mere drop in the literary ocean for the force that is Helen Taylor.

Writing this book has been a real journey for me. I gave myself permission when I started it, to just let the words flow from me and do my best to not over analyze things. I have to stick to the advice that I am giving after all, don't I...

In some ways, it's been cathartic... In other ways it's really drained me. But then when I have been sat in a cafe, just letting the words flow from me, and there's perhaps been the smallest ray of sunshine, shining down on the laptop screen, everything just feels like it's exactly as it's meant to be.

I was even thinking to myself yesterday, how writing this book, has been a little like having a facial...

I've had a really good deep cleanse here, but at the end of it, I've come out smiling.

And working through this book is a little like that. This book has been rather like a facial...
A *facial for your mindset...*

***Which leads me to question... how do YOU feel
after going through this process, of reading
'your best kept secret?'***

You've gone through a whole range of emotions, the cleansing, the exfoliation and the hydration. So how are you going to maintain things, once the facial experience is over?

You wouldn't expect to go for a facial, then treat your skin like garbage and still maintain the same glowing results that you very first came out with.

So where do we go from here?

Will you pop this book on your bookshelf and then go about your life – as normal? Or will this book be something that has changed you, and maybe even inspired you?

Will you finally forgive yourself for all of those times in your 'past life' where you allowed fear or anxiety to control you? Or will you continue to live in fear, unable to step into alignment with the life that is meant for you?

Choose to face the future with firm determination –
and life will truly change for you.

You see, choosing to take the power back, is like
choosing to get that facial, it's like choosing to get those
fillers, or it's like choosing to get that thread lift. You're
turning to face your future and saying to hell with
feeling like crap about things!

YOU can choose how your life (and your face) will look
(and feel) for YOU. Only YOU should be the one who
predicts that. And even if life has other plans for you,
you can still choose how you're going to work around
that.

You see *that* is the real beauty in life...

The fact that *everything* is changeable.

No matter where you've been and no matter where you
are going – everything is changeable... You can choose
to change YOUR stories ending in the time it takes for
your heart to beat.

You can simply put yourself back in the driver's seat and determine your current destination. So tell me... Where are you going?

I hope that it's everything you want it to be when you get there.

Self reflection: Write your stories ending

Okay so I want you to grab a piece of paper, or get your laptop out and write the ending that you would love to see as YOUR life stories ending.

How would you want your life to be, to look, and to feel, when your each the end of it?

I know, some people may think that this is a little morbid. But I like to think that it's a little like goal setting. You need to look at the end result and the bigger picture so that you can then plan the steps to get you there.

Dare to dream BIG – what do you have to lose here? Let your imagination get the better of you, be as elaborate as feels good to you. Then, think of the things that you need to, the actions that you need to start taking in order to get yourself there.

This doesn't have to just be about your entire life story by the way. You can use this exercise for a short period of time too, perhaps to get over a breakup or launch a new business. Look at the end result ... what is it that you want to see there, who do you want to be there, how do you want to feel. And then feel it as if you already ARE there... the Universe will respond to that.

#justforme...

Make notes **#justforyou** so that you can remember any moments of inspiration, a-ha's and breakthroughs that this chapter gave to you:

_____

_____

_____

_____

_____

_____

_____

_____

_____

_____

_____

A final touch of taylormade therapy

Today, as we come towards the end of this book, I want you to create an at home spa treatment. This means, fill the bath and add an oil that is relaxing.

Be sure to light a candle... And treat yourself to an all over body scrub.

If a glass of wine is your thing, then pour yourself a nice chilled glass of that... and for heaven's sake *turn your phone off.*

Then step into the bath and unwind for a bit, and think about this journey, Of all of the ahas and the funny moments. Of all of the breakthroughs and 'OMG' bits.

Take a look back at the #justforme pages – has any of what's come out surprised you? Or did you deep down really already know all of this?

The fact is that we usually already know it – but sometimes we just need a reminder.

A gentle, loving reminder, that life is yours to tailor. YOU, and nobody else, can create your life to be exactly as you want it. YOU and nobody else can design a life that is *bespoke.*

It doesn't matter what the past had in store for you – you can CHOOSE how to taylormake things in a way that works for YOU. Got a bad memory that you just can't seem to get over? CHOOSE how you want to reframe that.

You see, I honestly believe that we can learn a lesson from everything – and that we can turn any negative into a positive. Even if life seems to have it in for you, you can choose how you *act* or *react* to things.

YOU are the one in control here and nobody can ever take YOU away from you. Never. Ever...

Never

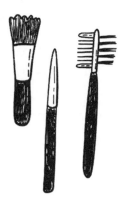

#justforyou – #justforme

So as we reach the end of this book,
I wanted to take a moment to thank you.

It's been a really soul searching journey for me.

Having you here, reading this, well it really means a lot
to me. There have been times when I have been sat
writing this, I that I have found it hard to deal with.

Seeing your life noted down on paper, can somehow
make things – seem that bit more real. Does that sound
a little bit strange to you?

I have had moments where I have felt liberated in unearthing some of these memories... and have thoroughly enjoyed being able to share them with you... and then I have had moments of sheer panic – where I have deleted entire chapters, and been kept awake at night wondering 'should I *actually* write that?'

In the end, I decided to take my own advice on things – to feel the fear and to just jump right in and do it. To refuse to over analyze it... to just make a choice to go for it, and then DO IT.

And as a result of that decision, I am sitting here writing this last chapter. I almost don't want to end this, because I've become fond of having your company.

I hope that this book has given something to you – whether it's the odd laugh here, or the odd tear there. I really hope that somehow, even if in just the smallest way, that this book has somehow inspired you.

Inspired you...

To go out there and be the YOU who is currently in there.

And reminded you...

Of the YOU who has always been there.

Agdin, thank you, from the bottom of my heart, for always being there beside me. Whether it's as a friendly follower on Facebook, or a loyal client at the Clinic. Just knowing that a woman such as you is by my side, makes this journey through life that much brighter.

I want to end this book by dedicating it to you. The you as a little girl, as a teenager, and as a woman. And I want to dedicate this book to ME. To the real Helen Taylor. Who has always been much stronger than she thought, it just took this book for her to realise.

This book, I hope has become your best kept secret, and I wrote it #justforyou because I needed to #justforme.

Until the next time,

Take Care,

Helen

xxx